LIFE
Rock & Roll at 50

LIFE

Editor Robert Sullivan
Creative Director Ian Denning
Picture Editor Barbara Baker Burrows
Senior Editor Robert Andreas
Associate Picture Editor Christina Lieberman
Writer/Reporter Megan Kaplan
Copy Pam Warren (Chief), J.C. Choi
Consulting Editors Christopher John Farley, Benjamin Nugent
Production Manager Michael Roseman
Picture Research Lauren Steel, Sarah Burrows

General Manager Andrew Blau
Finance Director Camille Sanabria

Time Inc. Home Entertainment

President Rob Gursha
Vice President, Branded Businesses David Arfine
Executive Director, Marketing Services Carol Pittard
Director, Retail & Special Sales Tom Mifsud
Director of Finance Tricia Griffin
Marketing Director Kenneth Maehlum
Assistant Director Ann Marie Ross
Prepress Manager Emily Rabin
Associate Product Manager Jennifer Dowell
Assistant Product Manager Michelle Kuhr

Special thanks to:
Suzanne DeBenedetto, Robert Dente, Gina Di Meglio, Peter Harper, Natalie McCrea, Jessica McGrath, Jonathan Polsky, Mary Jane Rigoroso, Steven Sandonato, Meredith Shelley, Bozena Szwagulinski, Marina Weinstein, Niki Whelan

Published by

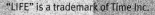

LIFE Books

Time Inc.
1271 Avenue of the Americas
New York, New York 10020

Library of Congress Control Number: 2002100178
ISBN: 1-929049-49-8

©Alfred Wertheimer

50 Years of Rock and Roll

By Dick Clark

Jack Stager//Globe Photos

Nineteen fifty-two. That was quite a year.

Deejay and promoter Alan Freed had his Moondog Coronation Ball in Cleveland Arena on March 21. Some say that was the first rock 'n' roll stage show. When the crowd stormed the doors, it certainly became the first rock 'n' roll riot. Lloyd Price's "Lawdy Miss Clawdy" started picking up white buyers as well as black in 1952. Down in Memphis, producer Sam Phillips started his Sun label that

year. Up in Philadelphia, where I was at the time, a new afternoon show began on WFIL-TV. Hosts Bob Horn and Lee Stewart called it *Bandstand,* and it was instantly popular. I was an announcer at WFIL's radio and TV stations and didn't have anything to do with *Bandstand* right away. But I could tell something was happening in 1952 . . . 50 years ago . . . if you can believe it!

I had grown up in Mount Vernon, N.Y., and had wanted to be in radio since I was 13. Rhythm and blues wasn't widely popular yet, never mind rock 'n' roll. I was drawn to big band music vocalists. I dated a girl in high school who liked jazz. Through her, I sort of got in sideways to black music. I loved rhythm and blues.

I got a job at the campus radio station when I went to Syracuse University, then the job in Philly, just as things were about to change. Kids were embracing a new form of music and it just could not be stopped, not that people didn't try. I've got a couple of quotes here. One is from U.S. Congressman Emanuel Celler, who said at a government hearing in the mid-1950s, "Well . . . rock and roll has its place, there's no question about it. It's given great impetus to talent, particularly among the colored people. It's a natural expression of their emotions and gyrations." Then he went on to say that in his considered opinion, however, these "animal gyrations" and the music itself "caters to bad taste." The songwriter Billy Rose also testified at

Paul Schutzer

that hearing and enthusiastically agreed with Celler that most of the new songs were "junk . . . in many cases they are obscene junk pretty much on a level with dirty comic magazines." Rose saw rock 'n' rollers as "a set of untalented twisters and twitchers whose appeal is largely to the zootsuiter and the juvenile delinquent." This was from the man who gave us the lyrics "Barney Google, with the goo-goo-googly eyes."

But as I say, there was no stopping rock 'n' roll. We could see this at WFIL. *Bandstand* was supposed to be a musical film show, but the kids got bored just watching the film clips and got up and danced. The station started bringing singers into the studio to lip-synch their hits. Suddenly, *Bandstand* was the most popular show in the city and the most exciting. I was lucky enough to become host of the show in 1956. When we took it nationally on ABC soon thereafter, we had a phenomenon on our hands.

Those were great years. We had Chuck Berry on the show, Fats Domino, the Everly Brothers, Bill Haley, Dion and the Belmonts. Elvis never played *American Bandstand,* but I certainly do remember the first time I saw Elvis, at the arena in Philadelphia at 46th and Market. I knew he was something bigger than life. I can remember it now . . . you were absolutely unable to hear the music for all the screaming!

I was not impressed with the Beatles at first, nor was the *Bandstand* audience. "She Loves You" had come out on the Swan label. We put it on "Rate-a-Record" and gave it a spin. The kids gave it a 73 rating . . . not too good. I thought the Beatles were essentially a British bar band, something out of Buddy Holly. But, of course, as they evolved, they changed everything. They wrote their own songs, they painted pictures musically, they did concept albums . . . They took '50s rock and roll and added strings, new percussion, jazz, folk. They expanded all boundaries.

I wasn't a part of the psychedelic drug period . . . I smoked and drank, but I sure didn't need another vice! Nevertheless, on *Bandstand* we debuted Jefferson Airplane, the Mamas and the Papas, the Doors. I remember Jim Morrison really didn't want to be there. His manager brought the Doors on *American Bandstand* as a favor. Some of the music I loved, some I didn't.

A short time ago I bumped into Grace Slick in a supermarket line in Malibu, and I asked her about those days. I asked her if she remembered the Airplane playing *Bandstand.* "I don't remember anything about the '60s," she laughed.

Rock just kept lasting . . . it has now stayed longer at the top than any other form of popular music. When I speak of rock, I am referring to its lineage and to its continuing influence. Little Richard inspired Elvis Presley, who in turn influenced Michael Jackson and Prince. Those two certainly have had a huge impact on today's music. The boy bands and Britney Spears owe everything to rock 'n' roll. Entertainers like Garth Brooks were influenced as much by Kiss and Aerosmith as by George Strait.

Through this half century of exciting evolution, there have been many chroniclers of rock 'n' roll. One who has been there since the beginning is LIFE. I think the volume you hold in your hands proves once more that when it comes to capturing America in pictures . . . freezing a moment or institution in time . . . no one does it like LIFE. The thrill of rock 'n' roll is in these pages.

I've always felt that music is visual. I've said for years that "Music is the soundtrack of your life." Listening to it spurs memories . . . that's when you fell in love; that's when you graduated from school; that's when you got that job; and that's when you lost that job. The pictures on these pages, for me, work the same way. Let your eyes float over them and you hear the music playing.

The Top 100 Rock & Rollers of All Time

Every kid who has ever spent Friday night at a concert or a dance, or been mesmerized by the light of a jukebox, has his or her own Top 100. And it's safe to say that no two Top 100s are alike. The fun is in the fighting. What do you mean Jimi's not No. 1? Hey, where's Britney? Of LIFE's Top 100 we can say only this for certain: They rocked our world. We're betting a lot of them rocked yours.

Stan Wayman

Elvis Presley

1 In the 20th century, only a few individuals in the world of popular music were so far above and beyond what surrounded them that they became stars of a different, greater magnitude. Bing Crosby was one, so was Frank Sinatra. The third member of that tiny but brilliant constellation was a young man who emerged from a hardscrabble Mississippi background to become a phenomenon that may have been the biggest of them all—Elvis.

In his early years he was a sponge, taking in gospel and rhythm and blues, the Grand Ole Opry and Dean Martin. He was fawned over by his beloved mother, who knew that hers was a special boy: His twin brother had died at birth. Elvis, too, felt different, somehow special.

As an 18-year-old truck driver, he went to the Memphis Recording Service to cut an acetate disc for his mom. The studio's owner, Sam Phillips, eventually heard the voice and realized that he had his dream, "a white man with the essence of the Negro sound and feel." Yes, a genuine, unfeigned soulfulness, but melded with country and pop sensibilities. In 1956 the giant RCA bought his contract from Sun Records, and the fame rocket truly blasted off. Radio, television, motion pictures, Elvis was everywhere, and everywhere his look and sound were imitated. For most teenage boys, he was cooler than cool. For the girls, one look was enough. For adults, however, his hair, hips and lip were an alien presence that rankled, incurring above-the-waist TV images and the wrath of teachers and clergy.

Of course, Elvis survived and was a monster success, measured, for example, by record sales that topped one billion. Eventually, his sort of fame proved too much and destroyed him.

For some of his fans, one question lingers. What further artistic heights might he have reached if his brutish manager, "Colonel" Tom Parker, hadn't seized the reins? What excellent music and interesting movies will we never know?

©Alfred Wertheimer

The Beatles

2 John Lennon, never a falsely modest man, once said that without Elvis, there was no Beatles. Indeed, the rockabilly craze ignited by Elvis was the formative influence on each of the four young Beatles-in-waiting as they grew up in near-poor to middle class circumstances in the oil-slicked English port city of Liverpool. Without Elvis, the Beatles wouldn't have wanted to be what they eventually became.

The Beatles, energetic, electric lads that they were, took more naturally to the greased-back hair and leather jackets of their wild-and-woolly days in the Cavern than they would, later, to the neckties and collarless jackets foisted upon them by manager Brian Epstein. Beneath the moptops they were not, in fact, well scrubbed. (Lennon lamented that the Rolling Stones wound up with the snarling-rocker image, while the Beatles, veterans of the nasty Hamburg club scene of toughs and whores, were made to look like mama's boys.) Something else the Fab Four image hid: genius. It had to be something near impossible for adult America to imagine, as they watched the twitching and heard the screaming on the telly that Sunday night in 1964, that they were experiencing artists who would impact, advance and transform 20th century music in a way every bit as significant as what Stravinsky had done. Or Gershwin. Ellington. Monk.

The Beatles, in particular Lennon and Paul McCartney, were not just interpreters in the way that Elvis and most rockers before had been, they were musicmakers in every sense of the term, crafting songs with pen and performance. It's not so much that they laid down new rules for would-be rock stars; they exposed new possibilities. The years that have passed since John Lennon, Paul McCartney, George Harrison and Ringo Starr disbanded in 1970 have only served to confirm: There was never anything like the Beatles. There hasn't been anything like them since.

Harry Benson

Bob Dylan

3 In the mid-1950s a high school freshman in Hibbing, Minn., named Bobby Zimmerman, whose ultimate ambition was "to join Little Richard," formed a band called the Golden Chords. Thus began the astonishing musical journey of the one who, even before leaving the Midwest for New York City in 1961, had been reborn as Bob Dylan. At first performing in a style resonant of his hero, Woody Guthrie, Dylan conquered the world in stages: the Greenwich Village folk scene, the rock arena, the Nashville crowd. As the millennium turned, he was playing at special audiences for Presidents and popes, meanwhile creating new, vibrant music that continued to thrill.

He constantly challenged the status quo and through his genius revolutionized rock. His debut album in 1962, a folkie set, was followed the next year by *The Freewheelin' Bob Dylan,* which provided clear signals of what was to come with such Dylan originals as "Blowin' in the Wind," "Don't Think Twice, It's All Right," "A Hard Rain's A-Gonna Fall," "Girl from the North Country" and the antiracist track, "Oxford Town."

In 1965, *Bringing It All Back Home* featured a side of acoustic music and one of electric rock. Purists howled in protest, then booed him at that year's Newport Folk Festival and throughout his 1966 world tour with the band that would soon be called the Band. When psychedelia was all the rage, Dylan released the serene, country-tinged *John Wesley Harding* and *Nashville Skyline.* When playing arenas was the new thing, Dylan debuted his loose-jointed Rolling Thunder Review before 200 people in Plymouth, Mass. Whenever he was counted out, he released a new masterwork: *Blood on the Tracks* (1975), *Oh Mercy* (1989), *Time Out of Mind* (1997) and last year's *Love and Theft.* That collection crossed genres from country to rock to tin pan alley pop— pointing in all sorts of new directions. It was full of surprises, but coming from Dylan, it was no surprise at all.

©Daniel Kramer

James Brown

4 The most influential black artist in rock's history, Brown burst onto the scene in 1956 when he and the Famous Flames recorded "Please, Please, Please." Like many another, he had a gospel background, but he also drew on stints as a semipro boxer and baseball player. His stage shows were an explosion of jumps, splits and rapid-fire dance moves that earned him the nickname Mr. Dynamite. Brown put together a sensational band that included longtime members Maceo Parker and Fred Wesley. In 1965 he broke through into international stardom with "Papa's Got a Brand New Bag." For decades he was an important influence on music, and on a black community struggling to make its way out of the ghetto. His potent ballads and razor-sharp dance numbers had earned him their respect, and despite nagging legal problems, he continually passed along his pride and his style.

The Rolling Stones

5 For many they are, simply, the World's Greatest Rock 'n' Roll Band. In the early '60s, (left to right) Brian Jones, Mick Jagger, Keith Richards, Bill Wyman and Charlie Watts joined forces in London for music that was mostly covers of Chuck Berry and Chicago blues. While those influences would remain, Jagger and Richards soon became a team that wrote one great song after another. Watts had real talent on drums, Wyman was a decent bass, and Jones added his flair for all things new—until he turned up dead in a swimming pool in 1969, one month after leaving the band. For the Stones, drug busts and death only buttressed their image as rock's bad boys. Jagger remains the ultimate front man, a stylish singer and prancing Mephistopheles, while Richards, "the Human Riff," guides the band through the pulsating affairs that are their legendary shows. Their recorded legacy is immense.

Madonna

6 Christopher Ciccone once called his sister Madonna Louise "her own masterpiece." That she is, an intricately crafted figure of great rarity who may or may not be a feminist icon, may or may not be much of a singer, may or may not be a narcissistic empty vessel, but is one thing for sure: a rock star of the highest order, one with savvy, style and legs. Now in the 20th year of a phenomenal career, she has stayed unerringly on the beat while dancing from disco diva to Marilyn Monroe manqué to electronica queen. Madonna can spot the next thing coming a mile off, and she sidles right up to it, then she delivers it with full frontal force. She long ago perfected the art of creating controversy, which has been a powerful weapon in rock's arsenal since Elvis. She has done it her way, even down to creating her own record company and approving every artist signed, including star Alanis Morissette. Madonna can be pondered and questioned, castigated and criticized, but she cannot be denied.

Stevie Wonder

7 Stevie Wonder is one of the most "musical" people rock has ever known, musical in the sense that Louis Armstrong was musical, where the sound is always special. He opened everyone's ears when his third single, "Fingertips (Part 2)," and its accompanying album both hit No. 1 in 1963. His vital, inventive singing and harmonica playing made it clear that someone important had arrived. For the rest of the decade, he hit one pop homer after another, equally comfortable with gentle ballads or swirling rockers. Then in the '70s he kicked off a run of impressive albums that incorporated rock, gospel, jazz and world music. He later added reggae and funk to the mix. Some of the later love songs were a mite saccharine, but these are easily forgotten when one considers the likes of "My Cherie Amour" or "Isn't She Lovely." The list of upbeat knockouts ("Superstition," "Sir Duke") amazes. This is a man of profound musical vision.

Chuck Berry

8 He was rock's first poet, spinning three-minute sagas of teen angst that cleverly reflected that manic-depressive reality, whether it was the doldrums of school ("the teacher don't know how mean she looks"), the liberation of the automobile ("we parked way out on the Kokomo") or the allure of fine young things ("she's too cute to be a minute over seventeen"). Driving the lyrics were some of rock's immortal melodies, with guitar licks (and piano riffs from Johnnie Johnson) that remain fresh despite having graced the songs of a thousand others. His stage show, which resorted to local musicians to save money, provided a physical manifestation—leering grins, mock-defiant stares, the famous duckwalk—of his singular persona. It is difficult to say how much problems with the law, such as a long stint in reform school and two years in a federal prison for violating the Mann Act, informed his music, but we do know, as John Lennon said, "if you tried to give rock 'n' roll another name, you might call it Chuck Berry."

Michael Jackson

9 Born in 1958, he was already a member of the Jackson 5 by age five, and hasn't left the stage since—a fact that made him a star beyond measure and, meantime, cost him dearly. He has often lamented his lost boyhood, and cited this as a reason for his wistful, childlike personality. Jackson's enigmatic nature—some call it plain old strangeness, what with the oddly evolving facial structure and skin tone—often overwhelms an appreciation of his extraordinary gifts. His 1979 collaboration with producer Quincy Jones, *Off the Wall,* is one of the greatest-ever soul records, and its follow-up, *Thriller,* is a gorilla disc for the ages. When Jackson moonwalked to the gritty disco-pop classic "Billie Jean" on Motown's 25th anniversary TV special in 1983, he created a sensation—people were gushing about it the next day at school and work. Jackson's early videos led to must-watch MTV. His fame was global to a degree not seen since the Beatles, and continues to this day, even if aspects of the notoriety are unwanted.

Kurt Cobain

10 Growing up in a small town in Washington, he was a happy boy who loved the Beatles. His parents divorced when he was eight, and the next year Cobain became a devotee of heavier music: Led Zeppelin and Black Sabbath. (He once said that he hoped his band, Nirvana, might marry Beatlesque melody to Sabbath's power.) In 1987, Cobain and bassist Krist Novoselic began expressing their anger in loud, edgy, intoxicating songs. Eventually joined by drummer Dave Grohl, they released, in 1991, a disc that was the very definition of seminal. *Nevermind* sold more than 10 million copies in the U.S. and, in "Smells Like Teen Spirit," gave a generation its antiestablishment anthem. Neither success, nor marriage to singer Courtney Love, nor fatherhood could dispel Cobain's demons, which included heroin addiction, and in April 1994, he killed himself in Seattle with a shotgun blast.

11 Eric Clapton

CLAPTON IS GOD declared the London graffiti in the mid-'60s, as young fans fell under the sway of the earthy but gorgeously wrought guitar lines that he was then playing for John Mayall's Bluesbreakers. Clapton had earlier been the first of the three supreme guitarists (the others were Jeff Beck and Jimmy Page) with the Yardbirds. After leaving Mayall, Clapton hooked up with Ginger Baker (left) and Jack Bruce to form the first power trio, Cream. One of rock's great bands, Cream was passionate and fertile, but after less than three years, Clapton wanted to return to a simpler blues format. He moved briefly to the supergroup Blind Faith, then cut the classic *Layla* with Derek and the Dominos before settling into a mostly interesting solo career, marred by the death of his young son in 1991.

12 Crosby, Stills, Nash and Young

A collective as much as a band, CSN&Y is nevertheless one of the magnificent acts in rock history. Stephen Stills (far left) and Neil Young (second from right) had already made groundbreaking country rock with Buffalo Springfield, and Young was embarked on what would become a tremendous, enduring solo career, when CSN&Y bowed at Woodstock in 1969. Graham Nash (right) was a veteran of the British Invasion hit machine the Hollies, and David Crosby (second from left) was ex of the Byrds. The 1970 album, *Déjà Vu,* made them the biggest thing in rock. For a moment they embodied the era, harmonizing beautifully in songs of peace and love. Then they were gone, occasionally to reunite, often to create great music individually, but never again to be quite so fine.

The Songwriters

Used to be, performers like Chuck Berry, Little Richard and Buddy Holly—singers who sang their own stuff—were the exceptions, as a backstage industry of songwriters provided constant fuel for Elvis, most doo-woppers and other early rock stars. Today the equation is on its head, with a songwriter like Diane Warren, who has written hits for everyone from Aerosmith to Toni Braxton, being the aberration. But at the dawn of rock the generally

Brill kids King and Paul Simon were writers dreaming of singing. Tunesmiths Stoller (on the 88s) and Leiber harbored no such illusions.

accepted rule was: The singer is the song's motor; the songwriter provides the gas.

Jerry Leiber, a blues fan, and Mike Stoller, a jazz pianist, were 17 years old when they began their songwriting partnership in 1950. One of their earliest R&B hits for Big Mama Thornton, "Hound Dog," became a rock 'n' roll smash for Elvis in 1956. Presley also succeeded with L&S compositions "Jailhouse Rock," "Loving You" and "Treat Me Nice," among others. For the Coasters, Leiber and Stoller wrote "Smokey Joe's Cafe," "Yakety Yak" and "Charlie Brown." To the Drifters they gave "On Broadway," "Spanish Harlem" and "Stand By Me."

Doc Pomus and Mort Shuman composed more than 500 songs and also had hits with both the Drifters ("This Magic Moment," "Save the Last Dance for Me") and Elvis ("Little Sister," "Viva Las Vegas"). Pomus and Shuman worked out of Manhattan's Brill Building, the largest refinery in rock. Tunesmith tandems including Neil Sedaka and Howard Greenfield, Barry Mann and Cynthia Weil, Jeff Barry and Ellie Greenwich, and Gerry Goffin and Carole King stoked the careers of Connie Fran-

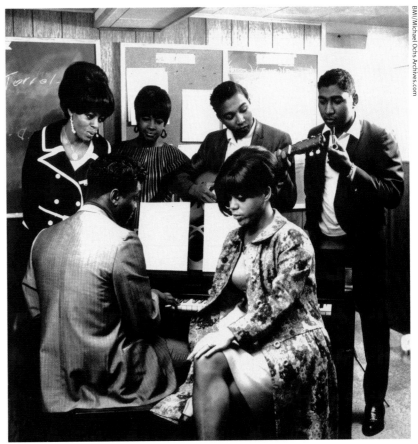

cis, the Shirelles, Little Eva, the Chiffons, the Righteous Brothers, the Ronettes, the Crystals, the Mystics and, yes, the Drifters. Conjure their songs and hear the Brill innovations: strings, Latin rhythms.

There was a whole lotta scribblin' goin' on elsewhere, too. Burt Bacharach wrote his requisite hits for the Drifters, then teamed with lyricist Hal David to pen a plethora of '60s standards, from "The Man Who Shot Liberty Valance" to "What the World Needs Now Is Love," not to mention all those Dionne Warwick hits, like "Walk on By" and "I Say a Little Prayer." Down in Nashville the husband-wife team of Felice and Boudleaux Bryant were polishing gems for the Everly Brothers, while over in Memphis, Isaac Hayes and David Porter built a stack of hits for Stax Records, including Sam and Dave's "Hold On! I'm a Comin'" and "Soul Man."

In Detroit the brothers Eddie and Brian Holland, along with Lamont Dozier, wrote and produced

The Philly sound was engineered by songwriter-producers Leon Huff and Kenny Gamble (top left). Working with Holland, Dozier and Holland, the Supremes were a sextet (above). Post-Dylan, the floodgates were opened and singer-songwriters such as Joni Mitchell, Gordon Lightfoot and (left) James Taylor poured forth.

more than a dozen Top 10 singles for the Supremes and also had superhits with Martha and the Vandellas ("Heat Wave"), the Four Tops ("I Can't Help Myself") and Marvin Gaye ("Can I Get a Witness"). Motown was a commune as much as a company, with Gaye writing songs for himself and others, Stevie Wonder doing the same, and Smokey Robinson being as responsible for the Temptations' success as he was for that of his own Miracles. What those three were doing was different from what "songwriters" had recently been up to. Yes, King had had a hit and Sedaka had worked his way into a recording career. But now a host of performer-songwriters were coming into the game.

Then came Dylan. And the Beatles. The gas/engine dynamic in pop music was shattered.

Some songwriters—Bacharach and David, Gamble and Huff with their Philly sound—persevered against the trend, but the new rule was: Write it, sing it. This rule has maintained, and today such as P. Diddy, who may start as gas, quickly turn into their own engine. For their good fortune they can thank John, Paul, George and . . . Bob.

13 Smokey Robinson

Famously called by Bob Dylan "America's greatest living poet," Bill "Smokey" Robinson is the architect of more hit rock songs for more performers than probably anyone else. At Detroit's Northern High School, he and four friends formed the Matadors, and after hearing them, Berry Gordy Jr. was so impressed by their sound and Smokey's writing that he decided to expand his nascent firm from one that leased out records to one that produced and distributed its own product. Thus began Motown Records, and Smokey (foreground) would become a v.p. That group became the Miracles. The brilliance of the songs he penned for other Motowners is astonishing, a legacy matched only by the man's singing itself. The master of a velvety, endlessly inventive tenor, Smokey ranks among rock's finest singers.

Michael Ochs Archives.com

14 Aretha Franklin

The greatest of all female soul singers, Aretha first recorded as a 14-year-old gospel singer while working with her father, the renowned Reverend C.L. Franklin. She then moved on to the R&B market, where she notched a handful of Top 10 records but found it difficult to break into the national pop scene. In 1966 she signed with Atlantic Records, where they knew just what to do with a four-octave singer who could get you up off your seat or send you to bed crying like a baby. Backed by the Muscle Shoals Rhythm Section, a sound emerged that would lead to such all-time soul burners as "Respect," "Chain of Fools" and "Think." Of course, Aretha was equally unrivaled with a ballad: Her version of "(You Make Me Feel Like) A Natural Woman" rests at the pinnacle of Mount Rock 'n' Roll.

FDR/Michael Ochs Archives.com

15 Bruce Springsteen

He is the common man as rock 'n' roll crusader. Wearing his sentiments on his sleeve, working past quitting time, giving voice to things his fans feel but can't properly express, Springsteen has, for three decades, enjoyed a very special relationship with his audience. Born in Freehold, N.J., in 1949, he hailed from a blue-collar world that would provide settings for his songs. He assembled a band that played a rocking brand of rhythm and blues, and they became heroes of the Jersey shore. *Born to Run* made Bruce big, *Born in the U.S.A.* made him huge. He has been a restless superstar, pausing on occasion for solo, Steinbeck-inspired investigations such as *Nebraska* and *The Ghost of Tom Joad,* or for personal journals such as *Tunnel of Love.* These only further unified Springsteen Nation. The Boss talks to them, tells them what he's thinking. They listen.

16 Jimi Hendrix

Rock's preeminent guitarist, he was held in awe even by the best of the other great axmen, who loved to tell of the first time they saw this incendiary magician. Born in Seattle in 1942, Hendrix began by backing such storied showmen as Solomon Burke, the Isley Brothers and Little Richard. Then in 1966, the Animals' Chas Chandler hooked him up with Noel Redding and Mitch Mitchell for the Jimi Hendrix Experience, and three smash albums. The Britons were a fine rhythm section, but Hendrix, a left-hander playing a right-handed guitar upside down, and between his legs, and with his teeth, and in every manner that had never before even been imagined, was like a visitor from another musical world. He later teamed with Billy Cox and Buddy Miles, and others, for legendary shows, but in its dreadful tradition, rock 'n' roll fame took its toll, and drugs 'n' alcohol took him in 1970.

18 The Everly Brothers

Born in Kentucky to midwestern country stars, they turned "Bye Bye Love," which had been spurned by 30 other acts, into an international hit in 1957. Coming shortly after the advent of rockabilly, the Everlys combined wicked country harmonies with a tight rock underpinning, often with Chet Atkins on guitar, to create yet another delightful sound in the very new world of rock 'n' roll, a sound that would inspire the Beatles, Linda Ronstadt, Gram Parsons and many others. For the next five years, it was an endless flow of hits, many of them written by Phil (left) and Don, including "Cathy's Clown," which sold more than two million copies. After that, there were successes, but the brothers feuded until Phil smashed his guitar onstage in 1973, leaving Don to say to the audience, "The Everly Brothers died 10 years ago." A decade later they reunited and have toured ever since.

Bill Ray

17 Ray Charles

The Genius has brought his incomparable talents to almost every aspect of popular music—jazz, gospel, standards, country—and rock is certainly no exception. Raised in Greenville, Fla., and sightless since about age six, Charles started out sounding like Nat "King" Cole, then got down with Guitar Slim before hitting it big in '55 with "I Got a Woman." While continuing to work in a variety of styles, he always came back to rock, creating such classics as "What'd I Say" and "Hit the Road Jack." An accomplished pianist and one of the greatest singers of all time, his work is always sophisticated while at the same time conveying the feel of a man who has definitely been there, done that. His vocal style shaped that of many others, including Joe Cocker, Bill Medley and Stevie Winwood. Charles has long been active in humanitarian causes.

Michael Ochs Archives.com (2)

19 The Drifters

They went through more personnel changes and more reincarnations than any other group, but in its first two decades this was a classy, able assemblage that bridged the gap between rhythm and blues and mainstream pop. The Drifters had more superb lead singers than anyone: Johnny Moore, Ben E. King, Rudy Lewis, Charlie Thomas. The greatest, though, was the man who started the group. Clyde McPhatter left Billy Ward's legendary Dominoes in 1953 and formed the Drifters to showcase his incomparably plaintive, stirring high tenor. In late '54 he left for the army and a solo career, but the group carried on and in a few years moved from the R&B charts to big-time sales with material from writers like Leiber and Stoller. In later years, there were countless groups calling themselves the Drifters.

20 The Beach Boys

Was it ever fun, fun, fun for (from top, left) brothers Dennis, Brian and Carl Wilson; cousin Mike Love and California buddy Al Jardine? Certainly not as much as it seemed. Pushed by the Wilsons' abusive father, Murry, the teens began putting surf-poems to note-for-note cops of Chuck Berry melodies, gaining a following but giving no sign of greatness. Then, in eerily beautiful ballads and upbeat concertos with intricate vocal harmonies, Brian began to show himself as a preternaturally gifted composer and producer. The song "Good Vibrations" and particularly the album *Pet Sounds* are exquisite pop masterworks, vintage 1966. But drugs and psychological problems took a toll on Brian, even as his brothers both died too young. Love and Jardine now tour in warring oldies bands, each claiming a sterling legacy not its own.

22 The Band

Richard Manuel, Rick Danko, Robbie Robertson, Garth Hudson and Levon Helm began to merge in the late '50s, leading to endless smalltown tours across the U.S. and Canada where they soaked up influences and congealed into a legendarily tight group. In the mid '60s they backed Dylan when he blasted into rock. These influences culminated in a handful of brilliant, seminal albums, amalgams of timeless rural mysticism and devastating rock musicianship.

23 Bob Marley

Even as the Beatles were becoming the rage in England in 1963, a group of young Jamaicans called the Wailing Wailers were storming the charts in their country. Marley, their leader, would go on to become a vastly influential cultural, political, even spiritual figure in his homeland. In the 1970s he brought the hypnotic rhythms and moral messages of reggae to the wider world. He survived a 1976 assassination attempt but died of cancer four years later.

21 Buddy Holly

One of rock's first singer-songwriter-guitarists, he was playing country music when he opened one night in his hometown of Lubbock, Tex., for Elvis. Soon Holly teamed with the Crickets and producer Norman Petty, and in 1957 began turning out delightful hit songs, each with a sound all its own. His lovely, playful voice and bright style have been a major influence on rock. His death in a 1959 plane crash was one of music's great tragedies.

24 The Four Tops

They were intact as a unit for 43 years, unheard of in popular music. High schoolers "Obie" Benson, "Duke" Fakir, Lawrence Payton and Levi Stubbs linked up in Detroit's tough North End in 1954 and worked their way through 10 lean years. Then Berry Gordy at Motown asked his brilliant producer-songwriters Holland, Dozier and Holland to kick down the door for the talented group. The solution was "Baby I Need Your Loving," the first of a string of classics that featured Levi's bracing baritone in poignant but pulsating tunes that were dance-floor magnets.

25 Grateful Dead

Emanating from San Francisco's psychedelic haze in the '60s, this former house band for Ken Kesey's Acid Tests embodied the counterculture for their diehard fans. Their fluid, improvisational music, ranging from amphetamine blues to lyrical folk, rarely produced hit singles but was often transcendent in concerts that, according to Deadheads, were best captured on homemade tapes. More of a tribe than a band, their long, strange trip ended in 1995 with the death of their troubled leader, Jerry Garcia.

Don Paulsen/Michael Ochs Archives.com

Herbert Greene/Robert Koch Gallery

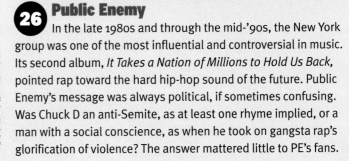

26 Public Enemy

In the late 1980s and through the mid-'90s, the New York group was one of the most influential and controversial in music. Its second album, *It Takes a Nation of Millions to Hold Us Back*, pointed rap toward the hard hip-hop sound of the future. Public Enemy's message was always political, if sometimes confusing. Was Chuck D an anti-Semite, as at least one rhyme implied, or a man with a social conscience, as when he took on gangsta rap's glorification of violence? The answer mattered little to PE's fans.

27 Sting

One of his generation's most abundant talents, he has acted in films and on Broadway while remaining a devout advocate of human rights and environmental causes. But it is as a singer, bassist and songwriter that this native of the north of England found international fame, first with the Police, a canny trio that blended minimalism, funk and world music in a series of arresting albums, then in an equally successful solo career that continued to draw on exotic rhythms while exploring deep personal issues.

Anton Corbijn

28 U2

Seldom in rock 'n' roll history has a singer so openly worn his emotions as has Paul "Bono" Hewson (right). Backed by Dave "the Edge" Evans's urgent, reverb-heavy guitar, his rock anthems of the 1980s—alternately personal or political, always passionate—first captured college audiences and then went wider. Perhaps responding to some critics' charges of bombast, the Irish band lost its way in the mid-1990s when it played around with chillier techno sounds and ironic detachment. Chastened, Bono and Co. delivered in 2000 the very-U2 *All That You Can't Leave Behind,* featuring the soaring ballad "Beautiful Day." The boys were back.

Alberto Venzago/Magnum

29 The Isley Brothers

If only for their first hit, 1959's gospel-inspired, frenzied-call-and-response all-time-classic roof-raiser, "Shout," this group originally from Cincinnati deserves plaudits. But the show—and their stage shows have always been high-voltage—didn't stop there. Two generations of the family (and friends) have continued to make hits across the decades in a variety of styles, from Motown to covers of white rock songs to disco to contemporary R&B, always with that Isley groove.

Frank Driggs Collection

Sepia magazine

30 Little Richard

Rock 'n' roll has always been about "New"—the New sound, a New look. And nothing has ever been more New than that moment in 1955 when Little Richard hit the scene, wailing bizarre lyrics while playing the piano from his tiptoes, and sporting turquoise suits, an insanely mischievous grin, mascara and a pompadour that high. For what had come before, Little Richard was Armageddon; for what would come after, he was the epiphany.

©Daniel Kramer

31 Janis Joplin

Born to a middle-class family in Port Arthur, Tex., she led a life characterized by vulnerability and isolation. Perhaps this painful combination prepared her to become the greatest blues-influenced female singer in rock's five decades. After a few false starts, she joined Big Brother and the Holding Company in 1966 in San Francisco, resulting in the classic album *Cheap Thrills*. Two years later, she formed her own backing bands for two good discs. Success proved an inadequate balm, and she OD'd in 1970.

Michael Ochs Archives.com

32 The Moonglows

Their sound was like a rich wind surging through a long, majestic cylinder. They called it blow-note harmony, and it lent their tunes an unmistakable sound. Alan Freed took them under his wing in 1952—their name derives from his "Moondog" radio persona—and they often appeared in his movies and stage shows as well as on his radio program. The group had two lead singers, Harvey Fuqua and the one and only Bobby Lester, and according to *Rolling Stone* "influenced virtually every succeeding black male R&B vocal group."

33 Tina Turner

Born Anna Mae Bullock in Tennessee in 1939, she went on to enjoy (much of the time) two of the most sensational careers in rock history. The first was as the wild soul singer fronting the Ike and Tina Turner Revue from 1960 until she finally left her abusive husband in 1976, fleeing a hotel room with 36 cents in her pocket. The second was her long but ultimately triumphant comeback as a solo artist. Her 1984 album, *Private Dancer,* sold 11 million copies, meaning that at some point even Ike must have heard "What's Love Got to Do With It" and "Better Be Good to Me." Her Wildest Dreams Tour in 1997 was sponsored by Hanes hosiery, and we know why.

34 The Clash

Not "the only band that matters," they were something just as rare: punk artists. Inspired by the Sex Pistols, they proved to be superior musicians and thinkers. The 1979 *London Calling* included everything great about the Clash: anger (damnations of racists, brutal cops and Thatcherism), a mix of styles (reggae, hints of rap), big thunder. They were punk Beatles, creative beyond all telling. Then, in the best traditions of the genre, they imploded. In 1983 singer Mick Jones (second from left) was booted from the band, whose next offering, *Cut the Crap,* didn't.

35 Roy Orbison

Blessed with one of the most beautiful, heartbreaking voices ever recorded, this unique songwriter-singer-guitarist took ballads of lost love to a new place; they were never morbid but always exquisite in their lilting misery. Of course, coming out of rockabilly, the Texan never forgot the beat, as on "Oh, Pretty Woman." His sad music presaged personal tragedies (the death of his wife and two of his children) and he endured a long spell of disinterest, but he was in the midst of a major comeback when he died of a heart attack in 1988.

36 David Bowie

He has had as many makeovers as Madonna. David Robert Jones, who started in the 1960s as a folkie, changed his name because Davy Jones of the Monkees had a claim on the original. Then he was a spaceman, then he ch-ch-ch-changed to Ziggy Stardust, then the Thin White Duke. He once said he was gay, then married supermodel Iman. If he didn't invent glam, he certified it—but he also led the way back to adulthood and suavity. Through it all, he made more than his share of smart, vibrant music. Thus, wherever Bowie went, many followed.

37 The Doors

Their name came from William Blake, by way of Aldous Huxley, which gives a good idea of the group's depth of purpose as well as its pretense. Jim Morrison's lyrics dripped with sex, death and politics and intertwined perfectly with the band's sinuous, foreboding sound to produce potent, eerie music in their first three albums. But Morrison was developing a serious booze and drug problem, and four years after their first hit ("Light My Fire"), he was found dead in Paris at age 27.

Mick Rock/Star File

Art Kane

38 The Four Seasons

When the big, bad British Invasion bands stormed the American shore in 1964, most domestic groups took to the hills. This was one foursome that just kept firing back. Originally out of Newark, the Seasons relied on songwriter Bob Gaudio, producer Bob Crewe and the Pharaoh of Falsetto, Frankie Valli (left). They had 50 hits in five years before changing tastes ended the run. In the '70s, Valli overcame hearing problems to run off another series of smashes.

Globe Photos

39 Ramones

Joey (second from left) died of lymphoma at 49 and Congress proclaimed May 19, 2001, Joey Ramone Day. Amazing. Some Queens kids form a band in 1974 because no one says they can't, get locally famous at CBGB for ditties like "Blitzkrieg Bop," never sell a lot of records but develop all the usual addictions—and their front man is honored by Congress. And by all of rock as well, for it was the Ramones, a unit of pure excitement, that juiced punk music. Without Elvis there is no Beatles. Without the Ramones there is no Sex Pistols, no Clash, no reprieve from 1970s MOR pop.

40 Otis Redding

Perhaps soul's sexiest male singer, he was one solid sender. He could render an achingly intimate "Try a Little Tenderness," then follow it up with a seriously volatile "Respect." He wrote that song, along with a host of other gems, including the timeless hit he penned with Steve Cropper, "(Sittin' on) The Dock of the Bay." This was a massive talent, a mere 26 years of age when his chartered plane crashed in 1967.

41 The Supremes

The most successful female rock 'n' roll group of all time, this Detroit trio notched a dazzling dozen No. 1 hits in the 1960s. Diana Ross, Florence Ballard and Mary Wilson all lived in Detroit's Brewster housing project and began singing together in high school. Berry Gordy liked them and had Motown school the girls in dance and etiquette. It was a good investment, as the aptly named Supremes emerged as a polished act that could perform in any venue. In later years, Diana became a solo superstar.

42 The Who

Throughout the 1960s, Pete Townshend and the lads made a continuous bid to be considered one of the Brit Band Big Three with the Beatles and the Stones. If the distance between those behemoth acts and the Who was considerable, the loud Mods certainly brought some valuable ideas and a lot of fun to the party. "My Generation" was a Boomer anthem, and in 1969 Townshend's epic *Tommy* became the first successful rock opera. Meantime, manic drummer Keith Moon introduced the idea of the exploding drummer to rock, while his mates in the front line refined the art of smashing guitars. In 1978, Moon overdosed on a sedative, and the band has never been the same.

Stevenson/Retna

43 Blondie

Like the Ramones, Blondie first developed a following at New York City's CBGB, then became big in England. In 1979, Deborah Harry and the boys finally conquered their homeland with the disco single "Heart of Glass" and the mélange-of-styles album *Parallel Lines*. Blondie was a pop band that dabbled in—and often heralded—the trends of its day: new wave, Europop ("Call Me"), reggae ("The Tide Is High"). Their huge 1981 rap hit, "Rapture," introduced much of the white audience to that genre.

Bettmann/Corbis

Jonathan Postal/Retna

44 Sly and the Family Stone

Mixing pop, soul, jazz and psychedelic rock, this Bay Area septet was the most exciting live act of the 1960s. Their multihued music reflected the band's lineup: men and women, black and white. While all the Family participated in the celebratory sound of horns, guitars and keyboards, the star of the show was Sylvester "Sly" Stewart (second from left), a sort of Soul Hippie No. 1. The '70s, however, saw the flamboyant Stewart tagged as unreliable, perhaps owing to drugs. It was the beginning of the end.

45 Van Morrison

Along with Dylan, he rules the legion of singer-songwriters. The Irishman staged his own British Invasion in 1965 when his band, Them, scored two Top 10 singles in England. Van the Man cracked the American scene as a soloist in 1967 with "Brown Eyed Girl," then proceeded upon one of rock's most beguiling careers. His 1968 album *Astral Weeks,* recorded in 48 hours, revealed elements of the inner Van: jazzy, mystical, questing, sometimes spacey, sometimes brooding, extraordinarily melodic. While the troubadour has at times wandered too far out there for the masses, to his fans the title of his 1999 CD, *Back on Top,* was wholly unnecessary.

46 The Shirelles

The first "girl group" to achieve star status, the Shirelles were four Passaic, N.J., teenage friends who sang for the fun of it when they cut the idiosyncratic, affecting "I Met Him on a Sunday" in 1958. With Shirley Owens Alston handling most of the leads, the group would record some of the best songs of the early '60s, including "Tonight's the Night," "Baby It's You" and "Foolish Little Girl."

47 Sam & Dave

Sam Moore and Dave Prater uncorked one of the most unforgettable songs of the 1960s, the call-and-response burner "Hold On! I'm a Comin'," and had a completely convincing way with a ballad. The majority of Double Dynamite's hits were done for Stax Records, backed by the crisp quartet Booker T. and the MG's. Sadly, hostility grew between the two men, and they split up in 1970. They reunited off and on, but the magic was gone.

48 Elvis Costello

Declan McManus was, in his first Elvis Costello incarnation, a punk—a 1970s new waver with a sneer, who sometimes drank too much and alienated audiences. Now an elder statesman of pop, he has created Beatles-esque masterpieces such as 1982's *Imperial Bedroom* with his band the Attractions, meanwhile moonlighting in various musical genres alongside collaborators like Paul McCartney, Burt Bacharach, the Brodsky Quartet and, since 2000, Swedish opera singer Anne Sofie von Otter.

49 The Velvet Underground

Co-led by Lou Reed and John Cale, the noisy Velvets, who released their first record in 1967, were the granddaddies of all art and/or punk rock. As a band, they died young. First the group ditched its sponsor and cultural mentor, the artist Andy Warhol (top), and Warhol's protégé, chanteuse-actress Nico (right). Then Reed and Cale's struggle for control rent the original VU lineup in 1968. More than three decades later, the Velvet legacy extends.

50 Prince

He was one of the reigning rockers of the 1980s, and an entirely inventive performer: exotic attire, narcissistic sexual writhing, trenchant singing, creative songwriting and a furious approach to his instruments. His music at its best was beautifully crafted, moving easily from pop to psychedelic to funk. Things began to get wobbly in the early '90s, about the time he changed his name to that of an unpronounceable symbol.

The Producers

Some are mentors more than anything, mothers and fathers coaxing the best out of their charges. Some are super engineers, wizards of the switches who create elaborate soundscapes. Some are connivers. Wheedlers. Some are cheerleaders. Some are hard-driving coaches. The best are a bit of all. These are the studio denizens who, in many cases, are as responsible for a record's sound, and the success of that record, as the performers themselves.

Sam Phillips did not invent Elvis, but he knew him when he heard him. In fact, he had already imagined him, the white boy who sounded black and could deliver R&B to a massive radio audience. That was the angle—producers often have angles—but Phillips, in the magical room in Memphis, also created the Sun Records sound, an echoey thing that was never muddy and that provided a striking setting for strong, manly voices like those of Presley, Johnny Cash, Carl Perkins, Jerry Lee Lewis.

Phil Spector's sound, brewed on the West Coast, was as different from Sam's as Mozart's from Mahler's. It has been called a Wall of Sound and it was that, a massive orchestral backdrop for girl group and soul classics. Spector would take a vocal, layer it with instrumentation and varnish the whole with reverb, producing a majestic gem. Quick examples: "Be My Baby," "You've Lost That Lovin' Feelin'," anything on the Christmas album—Darlene Love's "Christmas (Baby Please Come Home)," the Ronettes' "Sleigh Ride." Spector, more than any other producer in history, was the voice behind the record; his musicians were mouthpieces. Which is why, perhaps, his greatest failure is seen as the Beatles' *Let It Be,* handed to him for a touch-up during the band's acrimonious dissolution. Paul McCartney was enraged when he heard Spector's pumping up of "The Long and Winding Road."

Beatles music wasn't to be pumped up, it was to be . . . well, it was to be tended in the way George Martin tended it during seven years of brilliance. He was, truly, the Fifth Beatle, playing instruments, doing arrangements, hiring orchestras, helping Paul build his little symphonies and

Sun Records/CTSY Elvis Presley

Sun's Phillips had good reason to smile after committing the music of Elvis and his backup musicians Bill Black and Scotty Moore to wax in 1954. Spector, too, was buoyed when he took to the studio with the Ronettes—or Darlene Love or the Righteous Brothers—in the early and mid-'60s.

Ray Avery/Michael Ochs Archives.com

Frank Hermann/Camera Press/Retna

leading John through the mists of his psychedelic masterpieces. The early stuff was easy and could have been handled by anyone pushing buttons in London in 1963. The later stuff benefited greatly from Martin's inventiveness and classical training.

Danny Clinch

In what might have looked to be an unlikely alliance, the straitlaced Martin conspired at the console with the hipper-than-thou Lennon to lead an entire generation into new musical and social realms. Today, Lanois is one of several cross-genre producers, with a clientele including rockers, folkies and country cats.

Some folks look at these older examples and see a golden age of production, but the fact is, the golden age is now. Michael Jackson loads his latest CD with tracks from not one but four of the latest hot producers, each of whom has a sound. Bob Dylan likes what he hears of the Neville Brothers and hooks up with this Daniel Lanois fellow. Willie Nelson and Emmylou Harris, who years ago might have been wedded to the wonderful Owen Bradley in Nashville, also work with Lanois, while their country pal Johnny Cash continues the journey that began with Sam Phillips by making esteemed discs with Rick Rubin, best known for producing the Beastie Boys. The current stars of production—Glen Ballard, Timbaland, William Orbit—are today's Phillipses and Spectors, largely responsible for the sounds of Alanis Morissette, Missy Elliott and the new-millennium Madonna, respectively. As long as songs are waxed—or encrypted—in studios, there will be in-demand producers.

51 The Righteous Brothers

In 1964, this California duo went into the studio with wunderkind producer Phil Spector. The result was some great blue-eyed soul, like the plaintive "Just Once in My Life." But above all else was "You've Lost That Lovin' Feelin'," a soaring tune that became the single most played song in radio history. Bill Medley (right) was the guy who delivered the great low notes, while Bobby Hatfield twittered gleefully on the high end.

Ed Caraeff

Globe Photos

53 The Bee Gees

You could have won a lot of loot in early 1975 wagering that the trio of Brothers Gibb, erstwhile titans of late '60s balladry ("I've Gotta Get a Message to You," "I Started a Joke") but essentially unseen since 1971, were about to reappear in the limelight as the bare-chested, silk-pantsed, undisputed kings of disco. Never had rock seen such a remarkable—or more odd—renaissance.

Michael Ochs Archives.com

52 The Byrds

Harry Goodwin/Star File

The harmonies of Roger McGuinn, Chris Hillman, David Crosby and Gene Clark, rising above McGuinn's jangly 12-string and the steady drumming of Michael Clarke (second from right), were thrilling to hear in 1965 as "Mr. Tambourine Man" kick-started folk rock. Later incarnations of the McGuinn-led Byrds were alternately trippy ("Eight Miles High") and trad (*Sweetheart of the Rodeo*) as this great American band continued to invent new subgenres in rock.

54 Sam Cooke

He had started out as the lead singer for gospel's Soul Stirrers, but when "You Send Me" breezed onto the airwaves in '57, it was clear that a pure, new sound had arrived, and a singer in total control. He wrote a lot of his songs, which were as diverse as "Chain Gang" and "Wonderful World." Then, in 1964, he was shot to death in a seamy L.A. motel incident.

57 Santana

Carlos Santana's dad was a mariachi violinist; his son loved guitar and the blues. From the melting pot of Casa Santana emerged a Latin funk sound that, in 1969, forced rock 'n' roll to take notice of multicultural, otherworldly music. For three decades Santana led his band on musical and spiritual quests; fans were loyal, but sales were tepid. In the 1990s an angel, Metatron, told Carlos he was destined to reach a younger set. Was it Metatron or guests Lauryn Hill, Rob Thomas, etc., that caused 1999's *Supernatural* to be the biggest rock comeback album ever?

55 Led Zeppelin

As the Yardbirds faded out in 1968, their last guitarist, Jimmy Page, forged his bluesy riffs, Robert Plant's visceral vocals, John Paul Jones's booming bass and John Bonham's bad-boy drumming into the definitive heavy metal band. By 1971, mystical folk elements had been alloyed with their metallic sound. Their many hits include "Whole Lotta Love," "When the Levee Breaks" and "Stairway to Heaven." They disbanded in '80, when Bonham was found dead after an all-day drinking binge.

56 The Coasters

The clown princes of rock had a run of hits in the 1950s and early '60s. Working with material from Leiber and Stoller, the Coasters, who grew out of a group called the Robins, ran riot through crazy numbers like "Searchin'" and "Poison Ivy," usually with Carl Gardner as lead tenor. At the time, they were the most popular black group in the country.

58 The Sex Pistols

Their story reads, now, like a crude joke, but their songs and antics caused real-life mayhem. At a concert in 1976 their craziest fan, John Ritchie (nom de punk "Sid Vicious"), was involved in violence that blinded a girl. By the following February, Vicious was in the band (what a good idea!). The next year he was indicted for killing his girlfriend, the year after that he was dead of a heroin OD. Singer Johnny Rotten had already quit and the Pistols were done. A joke, or serious business? Listen to the urgency of "God Save the Queen" and hear a generation howling.

59 Steely Dan

Donald Fagen (left) and Walter Becker (second from right) met at Bard College in the '60s, and after trying different things, including a tour backing Jay and the Americans, they formed Steely Dan, which was the name of a dildo in Burroughs's *Naked Lunch*. Although they were never comfortable outside the studio—and a certain studiedness does color their work—their pop with jazz hooks and incisive lyrics provided some of rock's high points.

60 Wilson Pickett

One of soul's great swaggering stylists, he came out of gospel to join the Falcons, for whom he wrote and sang "I Found a Love." Then in 1964 the Wicked Pickett signed with Atlantic, and backed by Booker T. and the MG's he unleashed "In the Midnight Hour," a sterling example of his many rough-and-tumble hits.

61 Linda Ronstadt

One of the top singers of the late '60s and '70s, she really clicked with her third, self-titled album, backed by a group that would become the Eagles. Her career, however, has been hampered by two themes: Her choice of material is often suspect, and she never seems clear on a direction—rock? standards? country? Mexican?—thereby rendering them all just a little suspect.

62 Dave Matthews Band

Many dynamics of 1990s rock—noise, multiculturalism, a return of the singer-songwriter ethos—were on display whenever the DMB took the stage. Matthews (far right), South African born and New York bred, concocted jazzy world rock 'n' roll, reeds and violins decorating his propulsive songs. Theretofore famous for thrashing away at his acoustic guitar, he finally plugged in on last year's *Everyday*.

63 Talking Heads

With its origins at the Rhode Island School of Design, Talking Heads was one of the artiest rock bands ever. For more than a decade beginning in 1977, David Byrne (second from left) and the group explored African rhythms, funk, country, hard rock and soft. Theirs was music in a funhouse: the happy-go-lucky "Psycho Killer," Byrne's wacky vocalizing and bizarre stage persona—all those jerky movements, sometimes done inside a white suit two sizes too big. It is odd to realize that, finally, the Heads' often dense, frequently alarming music was one thing above all: catchy.

64 The Temptations

The choice of many as the ultimate black vocal group, they came together in Detroit in 1961 as the Elgins. After Motown's Berry Gordy renamed them, they found lasting success when they began to perform material written by Smokey Robinson, including one of rock's immortal ballads, "My Girl." Frequent personnel changes only enhanced the Tempts' ability to adapt to changing musical tastes, and they have continued to enjoy success in the new millennium.

65 The Allman Brothers Band

The voyage of the Allman Brothers Band, begun in 1969, is much like one of the group's blues jams: flowing, long, uplifting, sad. There are peaks (the early success in the South; the Fillmore gigs; the No. 1 *Brothers and Sisters* in 1973; the late-career comeback) and troughs (the early deaths of guitarist Duane Allman and bassist Berry Oakley; the squabbling and breakups; the drugs). The song plays on in 2002.

66 Paul Simon

Forty-five years ago a New York City teenage act called Tom and Jerry cut a single, "Hey, Schoolgirl," and enjoyed a modest celebrity. Having dropped the pseudonyms, Paul Simon (left) and Art Garfunkel hit it big in the '60s with a series of landmark folk-rock albums. They split in 1970, and Simon, who had always been the songwriter, went on to a long and successful solo career capped by his explorations of African music.

67 The Kinks

Early on, Ray Davies (left) rocked as hard as any British Invader, Animals included, on singles like the seismic "You Really Got Me." Then he was the melodic bard of English middle-class life on the gorgeous "Sunny Afternoon," "Waterloo Sunset" and especially "Days." Finally he was one of rock's patriarchal figures, with a massive oeuvre behind him testifying to constant artistic growth and more than occasional flashes of genius.

69 R.E.M.

Since 1980, Michael Stipe's cryptic lyrics, ethical preachments and increasingly strong singing have endeared this band of University of Georgia dropouts to, first, the alternative-rock crowd, then the critics and, finally, the whole pop world. R.E.M. has made several important albums, and Stipe, in the tradition of Lou Reed, Joni Mitchell and David Byrne, is an intellectual modernist worth listening to.

68 Marvin Gaye

His father was a minister in the Apostolic Church, and that music informed his early singing. After a stint as a jazz balladeer, he tried R&B and had a hit with "Stubborn Kind of Fellow." To some extent, that title described Marvin Gaye, who had his own way of doing things. Fortunately that way led to some of rock's greatest offerings, including his inspired teaming with Tammi Terrell. His father shot him to death one day before his 45th birthday.

70 Dion

One of the foremost white rock singers, his long career began with Dion and the Belmonts, named after a nearby avenue in the Bronx. Their hits included the sensational "I Wonder Why" and the anthemic "A Teenager in Love." On his own, he cut the classic "Runaround Sue" and "The Wanderer," but ahead lay a long battle with drugs. He would go on to make good, and varied, music, but the days of big hits were basically over.

71 Dr. Dre

As a member of N.W.A., along with Ice Cube and the late Eazy-E, Dre was a founding father of gangsta rap; the track "F--- tha Police" on the group's double-platinum 1989 disc *Straight Outta Compton* created immense controversy. Dre went on to a successful career as a soloist (*The Chronic*), mogul (Death Row Records) and producer (protégés include Snoop Dogg and Eminem). His influence has been vast.

72 Dusty Springfield

One of the most soulful of rock's white female singers, she set off a string of hits with "I Only Want to Be with You," and her trademark hair and makeup became a common sight in her native London. After a fallow period, she cut the highly regarded *Dusty in Memphis* in 1969; unfortunately it was a notorious nonseller. In the late '80s the Pet Shop Boys helped spark a revival, but the coming years brought a long battle with cancer that she finally lost in 1999.

73 Elton John

A flamboyant showman with a heaven-sent gift for melody, John had been trying for a half decade to break through when, in 1970, his eponymous album with its gorgeous ballad "Your Song" made him an overnight, transatlantic sensation. Through the years his weight, sexuality, stability, salability and addictions all went through well-chronicled fluctuations . . . but the music kept coming. Until now. John said in late 2001 that his last, fine album, *Songs from the West Coast,* was his final foray into the studio.

74 Curtis Mayfield

His incredible singing and songwriting were first displayed with the Impressions, and the lovely "Gypsy Woman." Increasingly, though, his focus would be civil rights, with "Keep on Pushing" and "We're a Winner." He went solo in 1970, and two years later did the thrilling soundtrack to *Superfly*. Disaster struck in 1990 when an onstage accident left him paralyzed, and he died on December 26, 1999.

The Disc Jockeys

Rock has always been about freedom of spirit, the quest for independence. But without the intervention of a certain species, the music's history would have been very different. The breed of cat we're talking about may be unable to whistle "Brown Eyed Girl," and there's an excellent chance they couldn't play a chord even on an air guitar. However, they know what music they like, and that is usually what we will like.

If Alan Freed hadn't heard that indefinable something that made his (and then our) hair stand on end, we might have spent the '50s hearing only the likes of Julius La Rosa, who had been brought to the fore by another talent hound, Arthur Godfrey, who then dropped him like a square bowling ball. But Freed had what any impresario must: faith. So he gave rock 'n' roll its name and a way to be heard—on his radio show and at his movies and stage shows. He talked to us, late at night, and knew what we needed to hear. Alan Freed lifted the music up and placed it in our laps.

Of course, others were into the sound. The "Ace from Outer Space," "Jocko" Henderson, had his *Rocket Ship* radio show that he broadcast in both Philadelphia and New York. A marvelous raconteur, Jocko loved to tell of the time someone was kicking on his front door at four a.m. "I put my bathrobe on, put my gun in my pocket," and found a fellow named Sam Cooke standing there, with a song called "You Send Me." Jocko played it, "and in three weeks it went to No. 1 in the country." He introduced a lot of great acts at Harlem's Apollo Theater, and once had to drag a shy Diana Ross out from behind the curtain. Jocko's whole style of rhyming patter and endless hippery helped mold the young music's ethos.

Murray the K was another New York deejay who influenced listeners, with his broadcasts for "submarine race watchers" and his holiday shows with top lineups. When the Beatles hit, he got the idea right away, and when they flew into New York, he cast himself as the Fifth Beatle.

In the '60s, Wolfman Jack had a show on a

Wolfman Jack was born with the no-frills name Robert Smith. Fans of his radio shows and TV work on *The Midnight Special* know why the name had to change. "Jocko" Henderson looks demure in the photo below; his *Rocket Ship* shows were a blast.

250,000-watt Mexican station that reached Alaska, spreading the word via his raunchy, howling humor and great selection of rockin' music. You could hear him in your car, on the front step, at the beach. George Lucas understood the role of the deejay, and in his 1973 classic film, *American Graffiti*, the Wolfman has a pivotal role, as himself.

By the late '60s, the deejay—that is, the disc jockey who spins records over the air rather than the deejay in the hip hop sense—was fading as a purveyor of musical tastes. The radio personality was being replaced by playlists, so that on-air talent basically told a joke and then played the song he was told to play (very much like the veejays who were to come). A lot of listeners turned to FM radio, where the sound was better, there were fewer commercials and there was a chance of hearing something hipper.

Colleges also jumped on the FM bandwagon around then, and today those stations are crucial transmitters of the music known as college rock. Once again, the sound of the new is being aired by people who know what they like, and what we will like, at least eventually. Rock's spirit of independence thrives, with a little help from its friends.

In the history of rock 'n' roll, Alan Freed (left) was as important as anyone. Host of the *Swingin' Soiree,* Murray the K (above) took over Freed's WINS prime-time radio slot. Below: Carson Daly began his veejay gig on MTV in 1997.

Brown Brothers

77 Black Sabbath

Inspired by the occult, Terry Butler, Tony Iommi, Ozzy Osbourne and Bill Ward took the blues-rock of Blue Cheer, slowed it down, pumped up the bass and added menacing, doomful lyrics, sending metal in a new direction. But in 1977, Osbourne (left) quit the band. He rejoined, then got axed in '79. In 2001, the original Sabbath rose from the dead to record new material.

Nitin Vadkul/Corbis Outline

75 Radiohead

Five Oxfordshire students joined forces to create the only '90s band that married iconic pop and self-loathing. With a textured three-guitar sound and vocalist Thom Yorke's anguished, enigmatic lyrics, their songs teeter between classic rock and futuristic electronic minimalism. In 1997, *OK Computer* made them a hot band that mattered. Then came the largely guitarless *Kid A,* the computerized *Amnesiac* and the raw *I Might Be Wrong* in a mere 13 months.

Bob Gruen/Star File

78 The Mamas and the Papas

The very best folk-pop group, they were a hybrid of Greenwich Village and the L.A. psychedelic scene. Their first hit, "California Dreamin'," evinced effortless harmonies and solid individual talents, also on display in 1967's autobiographical "Creeque Alley." By the next year, drugs, internecine romance and business snafus wrote finis to the eccentric, brilliant foursome.

79 Joni Mitchell

Roberta Joan Anderson contracted polio at age nine, and as therapy to help herself walk again she sang at night as loud as she could. That inner strength and commitment characterizes her music, which has influenced a wide range of performers. Quickly a success in the folk arena, she gravitated toward rock before delivering the classic *Blue* in 1971. In recent years she has made inventive, groundbreaking forays into jazz and world music.

Lynn Goldsmith

Baron Wolman

76 Beastie Boys

A rock generation before Eminem there were the Beastie Boys, the first famous white rappers. In the wake of their 1986 single "(You Gotta) Fight for Your Right (to Party)," a theme for the young and wasted, the Beasties showed an evolving sophistication, and their '98 release, *Hello Nasty,* had salsa and even opera in its mix. Surprising? Maybe not. Behind their pseudonyms, the Beasties are well-educated, politically active New Yorkers.

80 John Fogerty

In junior high school in El Cerrito, Calif., he, his brother and two pals started out as the Blue Velvets. Ten years later they were Creedence Clearwater Revival, the biggest band in the country, with rock-solid songs like "Fortunate Son" and "Born on the Bayou." They were a longtime foursome, but the whole show was singer and songwriter John Fogerty. Thirteen years after a heated 1972 breakup, Fogerty surprised everyone by storming back with the hit album *Centerfield*.

Baron Wolman/Retna

David Corio/Michael Ochs Archives.com

82 Al Green

Although plenty of singers have come from a gospel background, no one ever linked it so totally with slinky sensuality as did Al Green. One of the most individual voices in rock history, he cranked up the hit-making machine in 1970, but four years later a horrific incident with a former girlfriend drove him to enter the ministry. He since has confined himself mainly to religious songs but sometimes indulges in the secular.

Brown Brothers

David Corio

81 The Pretenders

Riding the new wave, Ohioan Chrissie Hynde, backed by three English mates, was as strong a personality as anyone in rock, and thereby a feminist icon. Her throaty vocals made the Pretenders' singles the most instantly recognizable on radio from 1980 through 1986, and even after the original lineup was in ashes—two of the four founders were dead of drug overdoses by May 1983—Hynde kept the band intact. It was a standout act on the 1999 Lilith Fair tour.

83 Fats Domino

New Orleans is, of course, one of the most fertile locales for music in the country. Its important effect on rock was first felt when Antoine Domino, who had been a major rhythm and blues player since the early '50s, made the scene in 1955 with "Ain't That a Shame" (which was covered immediately by white-bread Pat Boone, whose version greatly outsold the original). But Fats would have his day, as evidenced by his 20 gold records. The fat man is still performing today.

84 Martha and the Vandellas

One of the great girl groups, they were yet another jewel in the Motown crown. With a bolder, earthier sound than the Supremes, they turned several Holland-Dozier-Holland numbers into chartbusters. Lead singer Martha Reeves was impressive then and still sounds great. Some people consider 1963's "Heat Wave" to be the greatest rock 'n' roll song of all time.

Danny Clinch/Corbis Outline

Ray Flerlage/Michael Ochs Archives.com

86 Smashing Pumpkins

The Chicago alternative rock band led by Billy Corgan (second from right), one of the biggest acts of the '90s, made what might be called lavish grunge. On 1993's *Siamese Dream* and the 1995 double disc *Mellon Collie and the Infinite Sadness,* Corgan bathed introspective, often melodic songs in a guitar-drenched sound embroidered with violin, Mellotron and cello. The Pumpkins marked their era as much as anyone this side of Nirvana, closing up shop in December 2000.

85 Fleetwood Mac

Blues fans have little use for *Rumours,* the record-shattering 1977 pop album, much preferring the original, late-'60s lineup of grads from John Mayall's Bluesbreakers, called Peter Green's Fleetwood Mac (below). But let the purists whine. Numbers don't lie, and *Rumours,* a collection of tuneful tales from inside a band that was enjoying more than its share of sexual intrigue, sold more than 25 million copies.

Globe Photos

Steven Tackeff/ImageDirect

87 Kiss

That Kiss's brand of hard rock is thoroughly by-the-note, and that its power ballads are awful (remember "Beth"?), is not the point at all. The point is that the greasepaint and fake blood and fireworks of "The Greatest Rock 'n' Roll Show on Earth" have inspired the Kiss Army to buy nearly 100 million records since 1974, not to mention hundreds of thousands of comic books, masks and makeup kits. The size of the Kiss phenomenon is Alice Cooper's worst nightmare.

88 Jefferson Airplane

This San Francisco band really took wing in 1967 with their second album, *Surrealistic Pillow,* which showcased the singing of Marty Balin and especially Grace Slick, whose emphatic, druggy "White Rabbit" is a classic of the era. Other powerful albums followed, as the group, spurred by Slick and Paul Kantner, increasingly stressed political issues. In 1970 the band as such splintered, although the franchise would continue as Jefferson Starship, among other guises.

Frank Driggs Collection

91 Gene Pitney

"The Rockville, Connecticut, Flash" was not just another teen dream. He was the real goods, and approached every song with seriousness and intelligence, selecting his material with care. Pitney wrote as well, for himself and others, including "He's a Rebel" for the Crystals. The bulk of his hits came in the '60s, but he continues to produce, write and perform today.

Don Paulsen/Michael Ochs Archives.com (2)

89 The Flamingos

One of the most elegant of the doo-wop groups, the original quartet formed in Chicago in 1951. Their ethereal harmonies were heard early on the Chance label's "Golden Teardrops." Although they had a number of records that fared reasonably well, their biggest seller, 1959's "I Only Have Eyes for You," climbed only to No. 11 on the pop charts. Of course, quality isn't measured by sales, and their music is treasured.

Michael Ochs Archives.com

David Corio

90 Dionne Warwick

Her lilting, confident voice made some very challenging material seem ever so easy. The demanding music that she turned to gold again and again invariably came from the sophisticated songwriting team of Burt Bacharach and Hal David, who knew a good thing when they heard it. As she aged, her tastes turned mainstream, but bluesy takes like "Walk on By" have survived.

92 George Clinton

As a Jersey teen he formed a doo-wop group, the Parliaments, and he has fronted some collection or other—Funkadelic, P-Funk All-Stars—most years since. At first straightforward, Clinton's sound became eclectic, often bizarre, melding polyrhythms, screaming guitars, out-of-this-world garb and an argot all its own. The influence of Dr. Funkenstein on Prince, rappers and others is profound.

93 Tom Petty

"Refugee" was one of those singles that blasted from the radio, heralding a new contender. Petty had, in 1976, already recorded his Byrds-like "American Girl," which betrayed the Floridian's country leanings, but it was "Refugee" that made him a star. With and without his tight band, the Heartbreakers, Petty has made a lot of quality folk, country and rock music in the intervening years.

95 Beck

Beck Hansen hails from La La Land and a La La upbringing—his mom was in the punk band Black Flag and his dad was a street musician. This shows in his music, which is often fun, always fresh. The masterpiece is *Odelay* (1996), one of the great albums of the decade, with sounds, samples, soul singing and every flight of fancy imaginable. It is alt-art-rock at its zenith and shows that Beck is built to last.

96 The Eagles

Through the years many rock bands moved toward a homier, country sound as they "discovered their roots." The Eagles did the opposite, evolving from the laid-back early singles like "Peaceful Easy Feeling" to the concept cowboy disc *Desperado* to, ultimately, the sophisticated rock of *Hotel California*. In the process they became the biggest American band of the 1970s.

94 Björk

The elfin Björk Gudmundsdóttir is the biggest thing to emerge from Iceland since the Vikings. The former lead singer in the alt-rock band the Sugarcubes, which in the late '80s had been the biggest thing to emerge from Iceland since the Vikings, Björk has enjoyed a string of dance, techno and pop successes during her decade-long solo career. The little woman with the keening voice has also won the Best Actress award at Cannes.

97 Traffic

This quintessential late-'60s, early-'70s band was conceived by the multitalented Stevie Winwood (right). The four members secluded themselves in an English cottage, then emerged with a fairy-tale sound that blended rock, folk, pop and jazz.

98 Rage Against the Machine

Rap metal was invented when this L.A. group formed in 1991. Original front man Zack de la Rocha's father was an activist painter, and guitarist Tom Morello had a Harvard degree in social studies. Rage was happy to sign with a major label (and get total control) if that was what it took to disseminate their Marxist campus radicalism. Their seriousness has never waned.

99 Pearl Jam

Seattle, early '90s, appealing to college kids: Pearl Jam was a grunge band, right? Well, yes, but mostly no. Though guitars were indeed thrashed à la crosstown peers Nirvana, Pearl Jam—and particularly the vocals of baritone Eddie Vedder—owed a great debt to classic 1960s hard rock. On their more melodic songs, and there were a number of them on several exceptional albums throughout the decade, Vedder sounded like an up-to-date reincarnation of Jim Morrison.

100 Frank Zappa

For some an acquired taste, for others a genius unfettered by barriers. What is undeniable is that in more than 80 albums he considered nothing too sacrosanct to run through his zany social grinder. Zappa used rock, jazz, doo-wop, classical, exotic production techniques—and the kitchen sink— in his quest for musical and intellectual purity.

Is This How It All Began?

Trying to pinpoint the first rock 'n' roll record is tricky business, but in doing so, many musicologists pick a number called "Rocket 88." Here's the story of that disc as told by the man behind it, Ike Turner, to LIFE's Benjamin Nugent.

"'Rocket 88' was the first recording I'd ever done. I never had any idea that it would be called the first rock 'n' roll record in history. None.

It was 1951, and I was 20. My group, the Kings of Rhythm, played Greenville, Miss., every Saturday. We used to copy all the songs on the jukebox. Coming back from Greenville we would pass through Chambers and see all these cars parked there. Somebody was drawing all these people. It was B.B. King. We went in there, and he let us get up onstage. We played two or three songs and people kept applauding, bringing us back. B.B. said, 'Why are you guys not recording?' And we said, 'We don't know how to record. What do you do?' And he told me about Sam Phillips, and he said he was going to get him to call me. This was on a Saturday, and on Monday, Sam Phillips called me and wanted us to come up to Memphis to record that Wednesday. That was the beginning of it.

On Wednesday, going up there, it just looked like everything in the world was trying to stop us from making a record. We got arrested for not being far enough off the highway when we had a flat. Back then, they took you straight to court when they stopped you, and you paid the fine then or you went to jail.

We got going again. It was raining, and in those days we had to ride with all the drums and amplifiers and stuff, so our trunk was tied with a rope. That's why you hear distortion in the amplifier on the record—because it got wet.

We used to bet on whether we'd see more Chevrolets or more Fords on the road, and so this particular day, going to Memphis, since it was raining, I said, 'Let's bet on which car we see the least of.' I took Oldsmobiles. We made a bet on it. Then somebody in the group said, 'Man, what are we going to record when we get to Memphis?' We didn't know anything about original songs, we didn't have any. We just kept up with the jukebox. So in the meantime, this other conversation was going on about how many cars we were seeing. Somebody said, 'Let's do one on the Rocket 88.' Back in those days, man, that was the car. They had the 88 and the 98 Oldsmobile, and the 88 was superfast. Today you have the S500 Mercedes; that's the way the

Rocket 88 was in those days.

So we started writing it, and we all came up with the words. When we got to Memphis we went in and Sam Phillips looked at the words, and said we should move this verse to here or there. Then I started doing the piano, giving the guitar his part, the bass his part, the drums his part, and the horns. I wrote all the music on the whole song in 20, 25 minutes.

And we recorded it. It was a mixture of boogie with R&B, which people called 'race music' at the time. That's what made it what it was.

I had no idea what was going to happen with it, man. There was a white disc jockey in Memphis named Dewey Phillips. He had a radio show he was on called Red, Hot and Blue. He played the song. His whole audience was white, and, boy, they got on it, so 'Rocket 88' started a trend. That was the first time race music was played on a white station, and the record just took off. We had a hit that was accepted by the white audience. Everything got easier after that. That's where Elvis came from. Elvis started doing race music, and Jerry Lee Lewis started doing race music, and they went straight to the top—the whites that were doing race music.

There was no name for it, really, at that time. Then they started naming it rock 'n' roll. I wasn't thinking there would be this much stuff 50 years later about that same song. We didn't plan it, we just did it. I was just doing what I do."

Hey, Where's Ike's Name?

Look as hard as you might, you'll not find it on the historic disc. Two singles were cut in Memphis on the fateful day, March 5, 1951. "Rocket 88," the one that became the hit, featured a vocal by Kings of Rhythm saxophonist Jackie Brenston—hence the label. Brenston, emboldened by the song's success, tried to carve out a solo career, failed, became an alcoholic and died in 1979 at age 49.

Eras

B.R. Before Rock

In the primordial ooze of pop music, blues, country and jazz were aswim.

Rock 'n' roll, which through the years would splinter in many directions—folk rock, country rock, soul, fusion—had from its conception the DNA of all American music. Country music pioneers the Carter Family (below) were forebears of Bob Dylan, while blues man Robert Johnson and jazz queen Bessie Smith were progenitors of R&B.

Don Ornitz/Globe Photos

Star File

For boys who saw her on the *Mickey Mouse Club*, Annette Funicello was dreamy—plus she had hit records. Like Frankie Avalon and Bobby Rydell, Fabian was a Philadelphian made a star by Dick Clark. The Moonglows were one of the great vocal groups.

Ken Regan/Camera 5

Teen Dreams and Doo-woppers

Rockabilly cats, ersatz Elvises and harmony groups made the fans swoon and sway.

Soulsters and Surfers

Girl groups had us dancing in the streets, while California boys started having fun, fun, fun.

In the '60s, the girls started doing their share of the rockin'. Left: The Vandellas' Martha Reeves was a live wire. Dean Torrence (above, left) and Jan Berry (right), a.k.a. Jan and Dean, were pals with the Beach Boys, and they sometimes sang on each other's records. James Brown has always had one of rock's tightest bands.

Gene Trindl/Globe Photos

The British Are Coming!

As the Invasion wore on, Dylan, Motown and a thousand garage bands held the fort.

The furor touched off by the Fab Four was cause for much silliness as TV host Ed Sullivan donned a Beatles wig and, above, Mike Douglas was taught "the Freddie" by Freddie and the Dreamers. America's strongest response was issued by folkies such as Dylan and Joan Baez (opposite), while Paul Revere & the Raiders did their patriotic best.

Flower Power

Who can forget the
psychedelic era?
Then again, who can
remember it?

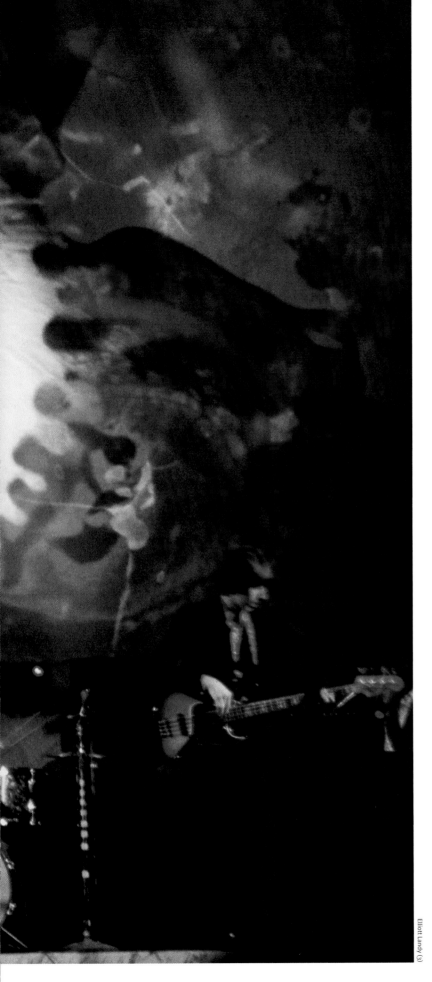

These photos, taken in the late '60s in New York City, feature the kaleidoscopic light shows that were de rigueur for many concerts at the time. Left: In 1968, the smart British band Procol Harum; above, some dazzling guitar work by Jimi Hendrix; below, Janis Joplin, soulful as ever.

Glam and Glitter

Rock was barely stayin' alive as the Disco Inferno raged and dancers shouted: "Burn, baby, burn!"

David Bowie has been rock's foremost chameleon. Here, in '73, he is Aladdin Sane. John Travolta, as a Brooklynite who lived to trip the light fantastic on the weekend, showed how to seduce a dance floor in the Bee Gee–studded *Saturday Night Fever*. The New York Dolls were puttin' on the ritz from 1971 to '75, miles ahead of their time.

New Wave Punks

Some were power popsters, some were punk poseurs, a few were truly dangerous.

In livelier moments, Patti Smith (below) helped jump-start a rock revival that was all about rebuttal. In the aftermath of the fatal disaster involving Sid Vicious and his girlfriend, Nancy Spungen, nothing seemed outrageous. After Sid was charged with killing her in 1978—and then OD'd himself—such far-out characters as Cyndi Lauper (left) appeared benign.

Frank Micelotta/ImageDirect

Neal Preston

For Queen and Journey and Genesis, it was power anthems that could reach the far end zone of a football field. For Ozzy and Alice and Kiss (below), it was Grand Guignol theatrics writ very, very large. For Bruce (right), it was a four-hour revival meeting sweeping across the land, healing the sick. For Madonna, it was . . . well, you know.

Lisa Rose/Globe Photos

Monsters of the Arena

The rock 'n' roll circus got wilder and wilder, and fans flocked to the greatest shows on earth.

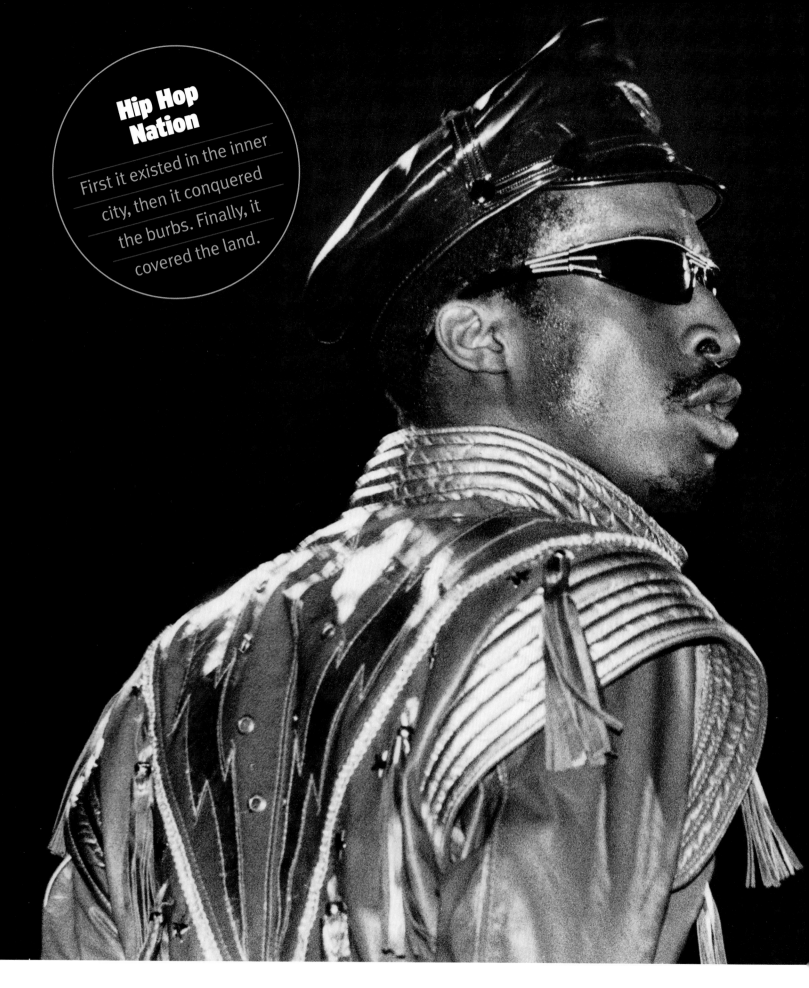

Hip Hop Nation

First it existed in the inner city, then it conquered the burbs. Finally, it covered the land.

In the '70s, Joseph Saddler, who had been born in Barbados but raised in the Bronx, began to master and embellish cutting, a complex art of record-spinning. Soon, as Grandmaster Flash, he assembled a crew that included Melle Mel and released the first record to make sampling important. Above: Chuck D of Public Enemy declaiming. Below: Eminem is hip hop's most controversial white rapper.

The Revenge of Kids' Stuff

It was back to the future as teen idols again took over the charts—and boys' and girls' hearts.

Rock 'n' roll is music of the young, by the young, for the young. In the latest wave of teen superstars, the **Spice Girls**, the **Backstreet Boys** and **Britney Spears** joined the **New Kids on the Block, Menudo** and **Donny Osmond** in the Fabian Hall of Fame.

Nuggets

When you go excavating in rock, you have no idea what you might find. Some gleanings elicit an instant smile. **"How outrageous! Oh, yeah, I remember that!"** Others are poignant, even sad. Almost all are colorful, the fashions as loud as the music. On these pages are several artifacts from the rock era that are housed at the Rock and Roll Hall of Fame and Museum in Cleveland. Photographed for LIFE by Brian Lanker

Alice Cooper's
Six-Inch-Heel
Leopard-Skin
Platform Boots

Roger McGuinn's
Mirror Shades from
his Byrds Years

Bruce Springsteen's
High School Guitar

Diamond Blessing

A Beach Boy's
Surfboard

Elvis Presley's
Blue Suede Shirt

Chuck Berry's
Orange Polyester Suit

Sid Vicious's
Bloodstained T-Shirt

D.M.C.'s Sneaker

The Temptations'
Stage Suits

Country Joe McDonald's Jacket

The Wrecked Fuselage of
Otis Redding's Plane

Jimi Hendrix's Velvet
Patchwork Jacket

Grace Slick's White
Leather Vest

Dance to the Music

As soon as rock 'n' roll struck a chord with the kids, its big beat pulled them outta their seats.

In the final years of the Before Rock era, dances such as the Congaroo (left) presaged gyrations to come. It was a very short leap from the lindy hop to the rock-fueled jitterbug craze of the '50s (above).

Julian Wasser

Walter Sanders

We're not sure what step the dancemeisters Kathryn and Arthur Murray were teaching here, but it seems likely that the folks above got their money's worth. The first half of the '60s was a hotbed of dance crazes, and the twist was the nonpareil. It could be rudimentary on the beach or Wallenda-like indoors.

Lynn Pelham

As the '60s continued, young people were beginning to "do their own thing." This freedom extended to the realm of dance, which meant that you could do whatever you wanted and it would qualify as dance. The people above were groovin' to some happenin' music in 1969 at the original Woodstock. By the mid-'70s, however, it was again time for terpsichoreans to embrace, which disco—albeit not for all tastes—made compulsory, as here at New York City's Studio 54.

Beginning in the '70s, and certainly in violent reaction to the tight rules of disco, things got way out of control. Punks at New York's CBGB (left) and in similar clubs in L.A. and London stomped and pogoed the nights away. Also of urban origin was break dancing (right), practiced in a club, a gym or on the sidewalk. In recent years, you needed some room for a decent mosh pit; never was there more space than at Woodstock II in 1994, where the mud pit was measured in acres.

Paul Schutzer

Rockin' the Box

Radio was rock's medium, but it played on TV, too, boosting Elvis and the Beatles, making the Monkees. Then, 20 years ago, came the cry, "I want my MTV!"

George E. Joseph/MPTV

Seeing Is Believing: Dick Clark started bringing rock 'n' roll to the nation in 1957. Teens could check out the latest acts, and the latest steps. Similar local afternoon shows sprang up around the country, usually with meager budgets and sparse sets. In the mid-'6os, NBC had a nocturnal *Hullabaloo* (above). Here, the Byrds are in their element.

A Really Big Shew: When Ed Sullivan saw the ratings Elvis drew for Steve Allen, he began a long practice of booking rock's biggest talents. Clockwise from left: Ed chats with Mick Jagger and a wary Keith Richards; Old Stoneface clowns with diminutive-but-big-voiced Eric Burdon and the besuited Animals; the King has an audience with bedazzled subjects; the Beatles (sans George) and manager Brian Epstein give a lesson.

The Beat Goes On: The Monkees were a poor man's Beatles, fabricated for the tube. Sonny and Cher had fun, and a good run, with their variety show. On *Hullabaloo,* Johnny Rivers sang one of his many hits.

Soul Train first got rolling in 1971. Its creator and longtime host, Don Cornelius, gave TV an urban-black-rock presence, with "the hippest trip in America." The *Train* is still chuggin' along. When MTV was born in 1981, the music business was forever changed. Above, Lauryn Hill on the popular series *Unplugged.*

It Wasn't Always Pretty

On the big screen, there were classic rockumentaries, the high spirits of **A Hard Day's Night** and the sharp satire of **Spinal Tap.** Then there were Elvis's 31 films.

Brown Brothers

Henry Groskinsky

Killer Couples:
Of Elvis's leading ladies, none came closer to matching his charisma and sexuality than did Ann-Margret, his costar in 1964's *Viva Las Vegas.* The heat generated by Annette Funicello and Frankie Avalon in 1965's *Beach Blanket Bingo* was of a considerably less steamy sort.

The Fab Three: A trio of fine 1960s films belonged to the Beatles. The best was 1964's *A Hard Day's Night*, which the lads, obviously including Paul (opposite), leapt into with gusto—a verve that came through onscreen. *Help!* (1965) was a slightly lesser affair despite the return of director Richard Lester. The Beatles were only moderately involved in the making of 1968's animated *Yellow Submarine*, but were happy to affiliate with the flick when it turned out to be a great cartoon.

Rockumentaries:
Woodstock caught
the spirit of the
1969 peace-and-
love festival in
upstate New York.
Similarly—if
horrifically—
Gimme Shelter
evoked the tension
of that same year's
Rolling Stones
tour and its
climactic moment
when a fan was
killed at the
Altamont concert
in California.

Mockumentary: In 1984, comedians Michael McKean, Harry Shearer and Christopher Guest donned wigs and became the front line of the fictitious, ill-starred heavy metal band Spinal Tap. Director Rob Reiner's brilliant satire proved that it is indeed a fine line between clever and . . . stupid.

"Rock Around the Clock"

In 1955, Bill Haley and His Comets, who had already covered Ike Turner's "Rocket 88," blasted off for uncharted spaces with that eternal entreaty, "One, two, three o'clock, four o'clock—Rock!" It was the first anthem for the nascent but already huge teenage audience that was Rock 'n' Roll Nation, as well as a dynamic theme song in the film *Blackboard Jungle*.

Bringing It All Back Home

Blonde on Blonde was the very definition of magnum opus, and its immediate predecessor, *Highway 61 Revisited*, is rightly considered one of the greatest-ever—and most influential—rock records. But it was here, in 1965, on his fifth album, that we first heard a rock 'n' roll band behind the Dylan lyrics— "Subterranean Homesick Blues," "Maggie's Farm"—and heard the bard declare "It's All Over Now, Baby Blue."

Fresh Cream

It's hard to say when rock got harder but fair to say that in late '66 this debut album by the brilliant trio Cream told us it was time to turn the volume up to 11. Cream opened the door for the quick acceptance of artists like Jimi Hendrix and, in a corollary, paved the way for lesser bands to gain success playing distortion-racked music. Their legacy is seen in the many permutations of today's metal scene.

Revolver

Before Brian Wilson of the Beach Boys and Paul McCartney of the Beatles staged their much ballyhooed creative showdown with *Pet Sounds* and *Sgt. Pepper,* this 1966 album showed the Fab Four had left behind the world of conventional pop songs and was starting to explore new realms. Rock was never the same.

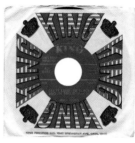

"Say It Loud—I'm Black and I'm Proud"

When James Brown said it loud in 1968, black people, young and old, listened, as the song provided a new kind of backing for a movement—black pride—that was already up and running. To hear a music god shout the slogan through the airwaves, in the very year Dr. Martin Luther King Jr. was assassinated, made real change seem within reach.

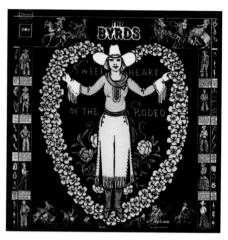

Sweetheart of the Rodeo

In the same year Brown released "Say It Loud," the Byrds issued an album that was the sonic antithesis of that song and all the psychedelia floating around, but was still very much in the realm of rock. Most heavily influenced by the band's newest member, Gram Parsons, *Sweetheart of the Rodeo* took rock 'n' roll down yet another road. To *Sweetheart,* with its sittin'-on-the-porch country feel, such followers as Poco, Linda Ronstadt, the Eagles, Loggins and Messina, Tom Petty and Wilco owe a great deal.

What's Going On

James Brown notwithstanding, most doo-wop and soul music of the 1950s and '60s was about baby love in the still of the night, or hearing things through grapevines; Marvin Gaye himself waxed his share of it. When Gaye came forth with this jazzy, introspective album in 1971, with its wonderings about the political and ecological fate of the earth, it was a revelation, and told all performers—black and white—to start thinking harder.

"God Save the Queen"

Talk about a backlash! Hearing disco, the punks blasted back. This Sex Pistols song caused the loudest commotion. It reached No. 2 on the British charts in 1977—during the Queen's Silver Jubilee—and set off an outcry nearly as raucous as Johnny Rotten himself. The nihilist Pistols weren't just attacking establishment Britain, they were attacking everything, and claiming they spoke for their g-g-generation. From the punks through Guns N' Roses to grunge and Garbage, loud, angry rock 'n' roll has never again been out of fashion.

"Like a Virgin"

Madonna had already notched a couple of club hits when this became her first No. 1, in 1984. Melodically it was just another pop song, but it sent an entirely different message than her earlier music had, and allowed for the rise and rise of women in rock 'n' roll. Madonna's persona, developed here and in "Material Girl," was now tough and raunchy. Most important, Madonna was definitely in charge. By the end of the decade, Janet Jackson could dance just as dirty as Michael, and Courtney Love could front a band every bit as loud and nasty as Kurt Cobain's.

Saturday Night Fever

The 1977 soundtrack of the John Travolta film was essentially Disco's Greatest Hits. For better or worse, this is the emblematic record of an era, a half decade when you sported an open-necked shirt, polyester pants, a flouncy dress and spiked high heels on weekend evenings. Yes, you did.

"The Message"

Grandmaster Flash was a pioneer of the turntables when rap was finding its feet. In 1982 he and the Furious Five, who had been rapping since 1976 and had developed a rabid following in New York City, delivered their message to the nation: Our culture is our own, it sounds like this, its concerns are these—violence, brutality, inequality, death—and we're going to express ourselves this way.

Backstreet Boys

This boy band from Florida first conquered Europe, and this CD, culled from two that had previously been released abroad, didn't become a multiplatinum smash in this country until 1998. At that point, however, it rang the bell for rock's latest round of teenage frenzy. The mania tradition dates to Elvis, Fabian and the Beatles, of course, and extends through Menudo, New Kids on the Block, Boyz II Men. However, it may be said that, as far as phenomena go, rock had never seen a kiddie invasion like the one spurred by the B Boys and quickly joined by 'N Sync and that dangerous mini-Madonna, Britney Spears. The next generation awaits.

Records courtesy of Val Shively (6), Howard Greenberg (2), John Tefteller

Moved to Mania

Since rock's prehistoric days, fans have been swept off their feet by their heroes. They raise a special din, matched only by that onstage.

Robert Hughes

Walter Sanders

The fans at right caught the rock 'n' roll fever early on: It's 1955, and they're at the Brooklyn Paramount for Alan Freed's Easter show. Above, in Seattle in 1972, the Rolling Stones clearly have this woman under their thumb.

Opposite: This teenager waited for hours outside the theater where Elvis was doing *The Steve Allen Show*. Moments before this photo, Elvis had paused and shaken her hand. Above: John Lennon watches as a member of the security team carries off a carried-away girl at the Beatles' final concert, on August 29, 1966, in San Francisco. Right: In 2000, a bevy of 'N Sync fans outside Universal Studios in Hollywood show off some all-world ivories.

Their Mamas and Their Papas

And their aunties and their uncles. Yes, music fans, rock 'n' rollers are human too—most of 'em—which means they came from somewhere. Here's where.

Globe Photos

From the beginning it has been fun to see those wild rockers in a family context—as here, when Elvis Presley sat with parents Gladys and Vernon. In 1971, LIFE asked John Olson to set up similar shots, and many of the pictures on these pages are his. Other photogs as well have taken this goofy tack, and their work abets Olson's in this portfolio of parentage.

Frank Zappa and parents Francis and Rosemarie posed for Olson in Frank's L.A. home.

Richie Havens with parents Richard and Mildred in Brooklyn

Joe Cocker and mom Marjorie at his boyhood home in Sheffield, England

Eric Clapton was raised by his grandparents and posed with "Mum" in the Surrey house he had bought her.

David Crosby visited his father, Floyd, at home in Ojai, Calif., in 1971.

Grace Slick dropped in on her mother, Virginia Wing, in Palo Alto, Calif.

The Jackson 5 cruised by the pool at the family spread in Encino, Calif., as parents Joseph and Katherine kept watch.

Kiss stayed anonymous, but the Stanleys, Frehleys, Crisses and Simmonses didn't, in a New York City photo shoot in 1977.

Ebet Roberts

Joey Ramone and dad Noel Hyman, in NYC in '89

Donna Ferrato

Bruce Springsteen with aunts in 1997, in his hometown of Freehold, N.J.

Keith Richards with children Marlon and Angela, and mom Doris, in London in 1982

Before Their Time

Rock 'n' roll, by its nature, is a dangerous trade. It is, then, unsurprising that many of its greatest practitioners have left us far too soon, victims of violence, accident, their own hand—perhaps fate.

Buddy Holly 22, airplane crash, Clear Lake, Iowa, 1959

John Lennon 40, murdered, New York City, 1980

Sam Cooke 33, murdered, Los Angeles, 1964

Jim Morrison 27, heart failure, Paris, 1971

Sid Vicious 21, heroin overdose,
New York City, 1979

Jimi Hendrix 27, asphyxiation resulting
from barbiturate intoxication, London, 1970

Janis Joplin 27, heroin overdose, Hollywood, Calif., 1970

Duane Allman 24, motorcycle accident, Macon, Ga., 1971

Otis Redding 26, airplane crash, Madison, Wis., 1967

Brian Jones 27, drowned in his swimming pool, London, 1969

Mama Cass Elliot 30, heart attack, London, 1974

Tim Buckley 28, drug overdose, Santa Monica, Calif., 1975

Jeff Buckley 30, drowned in Mississippi River, Memphis, 1997

Tupac Shakur 25, murdered,
Las Vegas, 1996

Notorious B.I.G. 24, murdered,
Los Angeles, 1997

Kurt Cobain 27, suicide, Seattle, 1994

Keith Moon 32, prescription-drug overdose, London, 1978

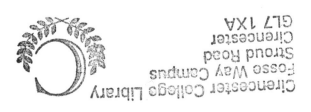

LIFE

Rock & Roll at 50